MW01268677

Created by Wild Pages Press 2017

Made in the USA
San Bernardino, CA
25 November 2019

60423893R00084